MICROSOFT COPILOT USER GUIDE 2024

The Ultimate Manual for Mastering the Features of this AI for Efficiency and Smooth Workflow

MARK O. HERBERT

TABLE OF CONTENTS

DISCLAIMER

The contents of this book are provided for informational and entertainment purposes only. The author and publisher make no representations or warranties with respect to the accuracy, applicability, completeness, or suitability of the contents of this book for any purpose.

The information contained within this book is based on the author's personal experiences, research, and opinions, and it is not intended to substitute for professional advice. Readers are encouraged to consult appropriate professionals in the field regarding their individual situations and circumstances.

The author and publisher shall not be liable for any loss, injury, or damage allegedly arising from any information or suggestions contained within this book. Any reliance you place on such information is strictly at your own risk.

Furthermore, the inclusion of any third-party resources, websites, or references does not imply endorsement or responsibility for the content or services provided by these entities.

Readers are encouraged to use their own discretion and judgment in applying any information or recommendations contained within this book to their own lives and situations.

Thank you for reading and understanding this disclaimer

CHAPTER ONE
INTRODUCTION TO MICROSOFT COPILOT

<u>Overview</u>

Microsoft Copilot is an AI assistant developed by Microsoft to support users across the Microsoft ecosystem. Built on the latest OpenAI LLM technology, Copilot enables professionals to integrate generative AI into their workflows. Microsoft aims to integrate Copilot into various aspects of its technology stack. Copilot is available for Microsoft 365 apps, Dynamics 365, and Windows, with a dedicated solution (formerly Bing Chat/Bing Chat Enterprise). At Microsoft Ignite 2023, Microsoft demonstrated its continued investment in the Copilot platform, announcing updates for Teams, Microsoft 365, and Copilot Studio.

Microsoft Copilot is an AI-powered assistant designed to boost your productivity within the Microsoft 365 suite. It integrates with various applications like Word, Excel, PowerPoint, Teams, and Outlook to offer functionalities across different areas:

- **Content Creation and Summarization:** Copilot can help you brainstorm ideas, generate different creative text formats, and summarize existing documents.

- **Data Analysis and Insights:** It can analyse your data in Excel or Teams chats, identify trends, and provide insights.

- **Task Automation and Workflow Management:** Copilot automates repetitive tasks and helps manage workflows across different Microsoft 365 applications.

- **Communication and Collaboration:** It facilitates communication by suggesting email replies, summarizing meetings, and translating languages.

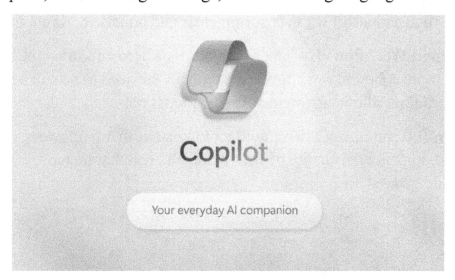

There are two main aspects to Microsoft Copilot:

1. **In-App Functionality:** This directly integrates with Microsoft 365 apps, offering suggestions and functionalities within the specific program you're working on.

2. **Microsoft 365 Chat:** This chat interface acts as a central hub, allowing you to ask questions and receive information based on your data across Microsoft 365 applications.

Overall, Microsoft Copilot aims to streamline your workday by leveraging AI to handle repetitive tasks, provide data-driven insights, and enhance communication within the Microsoft 365 ecosystem.

Importance and Benefits

Microsoft Copilot holds importance because it offers a range of benefits that can significantly improve your productivity and efficiency within the Microsoft 365 environment. Here's a breakdown of some key advantages:

- **Increased Productivity:** Copilot automates repetitive tasks like summarizing emails and documents, completing code and text, and suggesting replies. This frees up your time to focus on more complex and strategic work.

- **Improved Data Analysis:** It helps you analyse data in Excel or Teams chats, identify trends and insights you might have missed otherwise. This can lead to better decision-making based on real data.

- **Enhanced Communication:** Copilot facilitates smoother communication by suggesting email replies, translating languages, and summarizing meetings. This can save you time and effort while ensuring clear and concise communication.

- **Streamlined Workflow:** By integrating across Microsoft 365 applications, Copilot creates a more cohesive workflow. This reduces the need to switch between contexts and applications, allowing you to focus on the task at hand.

Overall, Microsoft Copilot acts as an intelligent assistant that empowers you to get more done in less time, improve the quality of your work, and collaborate more effectively within the Microsoft 365 ecosystem.

Target Audience

Microsoft Copilot targets a broad audience within the Microsoft 365 ecosystem, encompassing these primary categories:

- **Knowledge Workers:** This refers to professionals who heavily rely on Microsoft 365 applications for tasks like content creation, data analysis, communication, and email management. Copilot's automation and assistance can significantly enhance their efficiency.

- **Developers:** Programmers can leverage Copilot's code completion suggestions to write code faster and with fewer errors. This can be particularly beneficial for repetitive coding tasks or exploring new syntax.

- **Teams:** Teams that collaborate on documents, data, and projects within Microsoft 365 can benefit from Copilot's communication and collaboration features. It can streamline information sharing, task management, and project execution.

Here are some additional points to consider about Copilot's target audience:

- **Technical Proficiency:** While Copilot offers an intuitive interface, it might not be ideal for users with limited computer literacy or those unfamiliar with the Microsoft 365 environment.

- **Subscription Model:** Microsoft Copilot is currently part of the Microsoft 365 subscription plans, so it caters to users who already utilize this paid software suite.

Overall, Microsoft Copilot targets a wide range of users within the Microsoft 365 ecosystem who seek to enhance their productivity, communication, and collaboration through an AI-powered assistant.

9

CHAPTER TWO
GETTING STARTED WITH MICROSFT COPILOT

Prerequisites and System Requirements

Here are the prerequisites and system requirements to use Microsoft Copilot for Microsoft 365:

Prerequisites:

- **Microsoft 365 Subscription:** You'll need a qualifying Microsoft 365 subscription plan that includes Copilot. Not all plans offer Copilot, so be sure to check your specific plan or consult with your Microsoft 365 administrator.

- **Microsoft Entra ID (formerly Azure Active Directory) Account:** This account provides access to Microsoft 365 applications and services that work with Copilot, including Word, Excel, PowerPoint, OneDrive, Outlook, Loop, and more.

- **Microsoft OneDrive Account:** Some Copilot features, such as file restore and OneDrive management, rely on a OneDrive account.

System Requirements:

Microsoft doesn't publish specific minimum or recommended system requirements for Copilot because it runs as a service within the Microsoft 365 web applications and integrates with desktop applications. As long as you can run the Microsoft 365 applications on your device, you should be able to use Copilot without any additional software installation.

Here are some general recommendations for optimal performance:

- **Reliable Internet Connection:** Since Copilot interacts with Microsoft's servers to process information and generate suggestions, a stable internet connection is crucial.

- **Up-to-Date Browser (for web applications):** Ensure you're using a recent version of your web browser for a smooth experience with Copilot within Microsoft 365 web apps.

- **Supported Operating System (for desktop applications):** While Microsoft doesn't specify requirements, using a recent version of a supported operating system (Windows, macOS) for the Microsoft 365 desktop applications is recommended for optimal performance and security.

Additional Considerations:

- **Update Channels:** Microsoft recommends using the Current Channel or Monthly Enterprise Channel for Microsoft 365 applications to ensure you have the latest features and functionalities that work seamlessly with Copilot.
- **Admin Permissions:** Some features, like installing custom Copilot extensions, might require administrative privileges within your organization's Microsoft 365 environment.

By ensuring you have the necessary subscriptions, accounts, and a reliable internet connection, you should be able to leverage Microsoft Copilot to enhance your productivity within the Microsoft 365 ecosystem.

Installation and Setup

Microsoft Copilot is a powerful tool for increasing productivity and collaboration in Microsoft 365, Office 365, Teams, and other Microsoft products. Installing Microsoft Copilot on several platforms and applications

Downloading and Setting Up Microsoft Copilot

1. Visit Microsoft's website and navigate to the Copilot page.

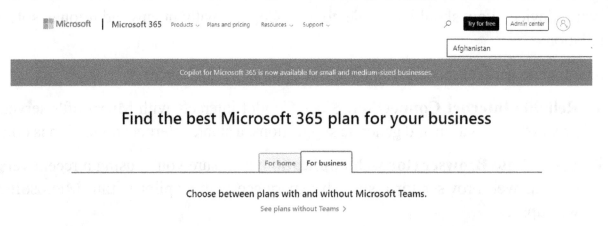

2. Select the suitable version for your operating system.

3. Click the "Download" button to download the setup file.

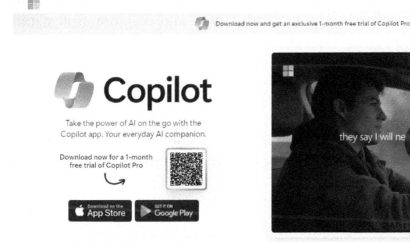

4. Run the setup file to install and set up Microsoft Copilot.

Installing Microsoft Copilot for Microsoft 365 and Office 365

1. Open the respective application (e.g., Excel, PowerPoint, Microsoft Teams).

2. Look for the "Insert" tab or the "Add-ins" section.

3. Search for the "Copilot" button within the "Add-ins" section.

4. Click the "Copilot" button to start the installation process.

Enabling Microsoft Copilot within Applications

1. Access the relevant menu or settings options within the application.

2. Navigate to the "Apps" section and select "Microsoft Copilot for Microsoft 365" to turn on the license.

3. For Microsoft Teams, sign in, navigate to the Apps section, and select "Install" for the Copilot for Sales app.

Installing Microsoft Copilot in Visual Studio Code

1. Open Visual Studio Code.

2. Click the Extensions icon or press Ctrl+Shift+X to open the Extensions view.

3. Search for "Microsoft Copilot" and click the Install button.

4. The Microsoft Copilot extension is now ready to use in Visual Studio Code.

By following these steps, you can seamlessly install and set up Microsoft Copilot across various Microsoft applications, enhancing your productivity and collaboration within the Microsoft ecosystem.

First-Time Configuration

Microsoft Copilot for Microsoft 365 is delivered as a service and integrates with existing applications, there's no complex first-time configuration required. Here's what you can expect:

Automatic Integration:

- If you have a qualifying Microsoft 365 subscription that includes Copilot, it should be automatically integrated into the web versions of Microsoft 365 applications you access through your web browser.

- For the desktop applications (Word, Excel, PowerPoint, etc.), Copilot functionalities might become available after you update your Microsoft 365 suite to the latest version. In some cases, there might not be a separate installation for Copilot – it becomes seamlessly embedded within the applications themselves.

Enabling Copilot (if necessary):

- In rare cases, Copilot might require manual activation within specific Microsoft 365 applications. You can check the settings or preferences menu of the application to see if there's an option to enable Copilot.

Familiarizing Yourself with the Interface:

- Look for prompts or icons within the applications that indicate Copilot's presence. These might vary depending on the application, but some common examples include:

    o Suggestion boxes appearing as you type

    o Icons or buttons that trigger Copilot functionalities (like content generation or data analysis)

    o A dedicated Copilot chat window within Microsoft 365 for broader interaction

Getting Started with Prompts:

- One of the key ways to interact with Copilot is through prompts. These are instructions or questions you provide to guide Copilot in generating content, completing tasks, or answering your questions.

- The Microsoft Copilot Lab offers helpful tutorials and example prompts to get you started with using Copilot effectively in various scenarios.

Exploring Settings and Preferences:

- Some Microsoft 365 applications might allow you to customize Copilot's behaviour to your preferences. This could involve adjusting the tone (formal, informal), output length, or how strictly it adheres to your company's style guidelines.

Overall, the first-time configuration for Microsoft Copilot is designed to be straightforward. Leverage the automatic integration, explore the interface, and experiment with prompts to unlock the full potential of this AI assistant within your Microsoft 365 environment.

Basic Navigation and User Interface

Microsoft Copilot's user interface is designed to be intuitive and user-friendly, allowing easy navigation and access to its features. Here are the basics:

Navigation:

- **Sidebar**: Access Copilot's main features and apps from the sidebar.

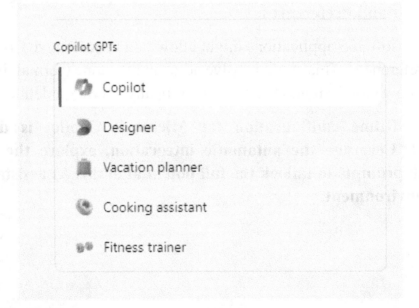

- **Toolbar**: Use the toolbar to perform actions and tasks.
- **Search Bar**: Find what you need with the search bar.

User Interface:

- **Cards**: Information and results are displayed in card format.

- **Chat Window**: Interact with Copilot in a conversational chat window.

- **Panels**: Access additional information and features in panels.

Key Features:

- **Home**: Start your Copilot experience with the Home feature.

- **Apps**: Access Copilot-enabled apps from the Apps feature.

- **Chat**: Engage in conversational AI with the Chat feature.

Microsoft Copilot integrates with various Microsoft 365 applications, the specific user interface (UI) elements might vary slightly depending on the application you're using. Here's a general overview of navigating and interacting with Copilot:

Common UI Elements:

- **Contextual Suggestions:** As you work within Microsoft 365 applications, Copilot might offer suggestions in real-time based on your actions and the context of your work. These suggestions could appear as:

  - Pop-up boxes with content completions or alternative phrasings while typing text (emails, documents, etc.)

  - Prompts to insert data charts or visualizations based on your spreadsheet data in Excel

  - Options for summarizing key points or translating text within documents or emails

- **In-app Icons or Buttons:** Look for icons or buttons within the application interface that specifically trigger Copilot functionalities. These might be located on the ribbon bar (top of the application window) or within the side panels. Here are some examples:

- An icon to activate content generation prompts for emails, letters, or creative text formats.

- A button to initiate data analysis or suggest insights based on your data in Excel or PowerPoint.

- A dedicated Copilot button to launch a chat interface for broader interaction with Copilot.

- **Microsoft 365 Chat Interface (Optional):** While Copilot primarily interacts within specific applications, some versions might offer a dedicated Copilot chat window within the Microsoft 365 interface. This chat acts as a central hub where you can provide prompts and receive information or complete tasks across your Microsoft 365 data.

General Navigation Tips:

- **Observe Contextual Cues:** Pay attention to pop-up suggestions or subtle UI changes that indicate Copilot's potential to assist you within the application you're using.

- **Explore Application Interface:** Look for dedicated Copilot buttons or functionalities within the ribbon bar, side panels, or menus of the Microsoft 365 application.

- **Utilize Prompts:** Craft clear and concise prompts to guide Copilot in generating content, completing tasks, or answering your questions. The Microsoft Copilot Lab offers examples and guidance on formulating effective prompts.

- **Review and Refine:** Remember, Copilot's suggestions are a starting point. Review them carefully, accept or modify them as needed, and provide feedback through upvotes, downvotes, or comments to improve Copilot's future performance.

By familiarizing yourself with these UI elements and navigation tips, you can effectively interact with Microsoft Copilot and leverage its capabilities to enhance your workflow within the Microsoft 365 ecosystem.

CHAPTER THREE
FEATURES OF MICROSOFT COPILOT

Real-time Assistance and Suggestions

Microsoft Copilot shines in its ability to provide real-time assistance and suggestions as you work within the Microsoft 365 suite. Here's how it enhances your workflow across various applications:

Content Creation and Editing:

- **Effortless Writing:** As you type emails, documents, or other text formats, Copilot analyses your work and suggests completions for sentences, paragraphs, or even entire structures. This can significantly improve your writing efficiency and reduce the time spent crafting content.

- **Enhanced Grammar and Style:** Copilot can flag grammatical errors or suggest alternative phrasings to ensure your writing is clear, concise, and adheres to your company's style guidelines.

- **Overcoming Writer's Block:** If you're stuck and unsure how to proceed with your writing, Copilot can offer creative prompts or generate different writing styles to spark new ideas and help you move forward.

Data Analysis and Visualization:

- **Smarter Spreadsheets:** While working in Excel, Copilot can analyse your data and suggest relevant charts, graphs, or pivot tables to visualize your findings effectively.

- **Data Insights at Your Fingertips:** Copilot can unearth hidden trends or patterns within your data sets, providing valuable insights that might not be immediately apparent.

- **Transforming Data into Presentations:** Export your data analysis from Excel, and Copilot within PowerPoint might suggest layouts, design elements, and data visualizations to create compelling presentations based on your findings.

Communication and Collaboration:

- **Real-time Translation:** Working with international teams? Copilot can translate emails, messages, or documents in real-time, fostering seamless communication and collaboration across language barriers.

- **Meeting Summaries and Action Items:** After meetings, use Copilot to summarize key takeaways and automatically generate a list of action items, ensuring everyone stays on the same page.

- **Crafting Effective Emails:** Struggling to write an email? Copilot can suggest greetings, closings, body paragraphs, or even entire email structures based on the recipient and purpose of your message.

General Workflow Management:

- **Task Automation:** Copilot can automate repetitive tasks within Microsoft 365 applications, freeing up your time to focus on higher-level thinking and strategic work.

- **Intelligent Search:** Utilize Copilot's search capabilities to find relevant information or files across your Microsoft 365 data quickly and efficiently.

- **Staying Organized:** Copilot might suggest ways to categorize your work, prioritize tasks, and manage your schedule within Microsoft 365, promoting better organization and time management.

Remember:

- To leverage Copilot's real-time assistance effectively, provide context through clear prompts and instructions.

- Explore the functionalities within each Microsoft 365 application to discover the specific ways Copilot can assist you in your workflow.

- Don't hesitate to experiment with different prompts and observe Copilot's suggestions - the more you interact, the better it tailors its assistance to your needs.

By understanding how Copilot offers real-time guidance and suggestions, you can transform the way you work within the Microsoft 365 ecosystem, boosting your productivity and achieving more in less time.

Integration with Microsoft 365

Microsoft Copilot shines in its ability to provide real-time assistance and suggestions as you work within the Microsoft 365 suite. Here's how it enhances your workflow across various applications:

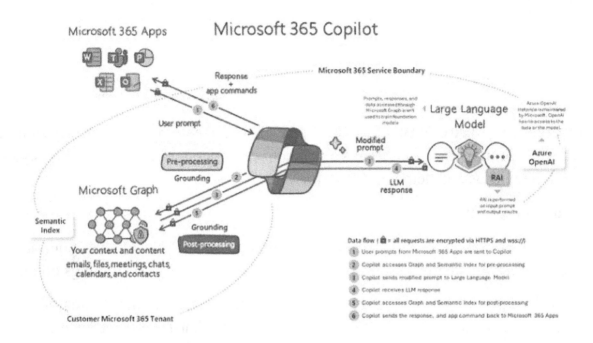

Content Creation and Editing:

- **Effortless Writing:** As you type emails, documents, or other text formats, Copilot analyses your work and suggests completions for sentences, paragraphs, or even entire structures. This can significantly improve your writing efficiency and reduce the time spent crafting content.

- **Enhanced Grammar and Style:** Copilot can flag grammatical errors or suggest alternative phrasings to ensure your writing is clear, concise, and adheres to your company's style guidelines.

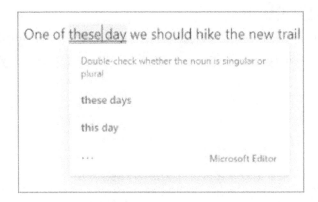

- **Overcoming Writer's Block:** If you're stuck and unsure how to proceed with your writing, Copilot can offer creative prompts or generate different writing styles to spark new ideas and help you move forward.

Data Analysis and Visualization:

- **Smarter Spreadsheets:** While working in Excel, Copilot can analyse your data and suggest relevant charts, graphs, or pivot tables to visualize your findings effectively.

- **Data Insights at Your Fingertips:** Copilot can unearth hidden trends or patterns within your data sets, providing valuable insights that might not be immediately apparent.

- **Transforming Data into Presentations:** Export your data analysis from Excel, and Copilot within PowerPoint might suggest layouts, design elements, and data visualizations to create compelling presentations based on your findings.

Communication and Collaboration:

- **Real-time Translation:** Working with international teams? Copilot can translate emails, messages, or documents in real-time, fostering seamless communication and collaboration across language barriers.

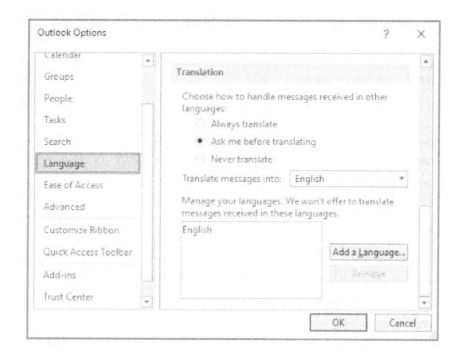

- **Meeting Summaries and Action Items:** After meetings, use Copilot to summarize key takeaways and automatically generate a list of action items, ensuring everyone stays on the same page.

- **Crafting Effective Emails:** Struggling to write an email? Copilot can suggest greetings, closings, body paragraphs, or even entire email structures based on the recipient and purpose of your message.

General Workflow Management:

- **Task Automation:** Copilot can automate repetitive tasks within Microsoft 365 applications, freeing up your time to focus on higher-level thinking and strategic work.

- **Intelligent Search:** Utilize Copilot's search capabilities to find relevant information or files across your Microsoft 365 data quickly and efficiently.

- **Staying Organized:** Copilot might suggest ways to categorize your work, prioritize tasks, and manage your schedule within Microsoft 365, promoting better organization and time management.

Remember:

- To leverage Copilot's real-time assistance effectively, provide context through clear prompts and instructions.

- Explore the functionalities within each Microsoft 365 application to discover the specific ways Copilot can assist you in your workflow.

- Don't hesitate to experiment with different prompts and observe Copilot's suggestions - the more you interact, the better it tailors its assistance to your needs.

By understanding how Copilot offers real-time guidance and suggestions, you can transform the way you work within the Microsoft 365 ecosystem, boosting your productivity and achieving more in less time.

AI-Powered Insights and Analytics

Microsoft Copilot goes beyond basic suggestions and real-time assistance. It harnesses the power of AI to provide advanced data analysis and generate insightful recommendations, empowering you to make data-driven decisions within the Microsoft 365 environment. Here's how Copilot elevates your analytical capabilities across various applications:

Unearthing Hidden Patterns:

- **Excel Gets Smarter:** Copilot analyses your spreadsheet data in Excel to identify hidden trends or patterns you might not have noticed on your own. Visualizations like charts and graphs are automatically suggested to illuminate these insights, making it easier to understand your data at a glance.

- **Data Storytelling:** Copilot can analyse data sets across different Microsoft 365 applications (Excel, PowerPoint, etc.) and help you craft a compelling data story. It can suggest how to connect the dots between your findings, present them visually, and communicate them effectively to your audience.

Predictive Analytics:

- **Forecasting Future Trends:** Leverage Copilot's ability to analyse historical data and identify patterns to forecast future trends. This can be crucial for business planning, resource allocation, and making data-driven predictions within your area of expertise.

- **Proactive Recommendations:** Based on your data and workflow patterns, Copilot can generate proactive recommendations within Microsoft 365 applications. For instance, it might suggest relevant information or files you might need for a specific task, anticipate your needs, and save you time searching for data.

Enhanced Decision Making:

- **Data-Driven Confidence:** With Copilot's data analysis and insights, you can approach decision-making with greater confidence. The ability to see underlying trends and patterns in your data empowers you to make well-informed choices backed by evidence.

- **Customizable Insights:** Copilot allows you to tailor the level of detail and the specific insights you receive. You can set parameters and guide Copilot's analysis based on your specific needs and goals.

Remember:

- To get the most out of Copilot's AI-powered insights and analytics, provide clear context through prompts and instruct Copilot on the type of insights you're seeking.

- The more you utilize Copilot's analytical features, the better it understands your work style and data patterns, leading to more relevant and personalized recommendations over time.

By incorporating Microsoft Copilot's AI capabilities, you can transform the way you analyse data and extract valuable insights from your work within the Microsoft 365 ecosystem. This allows you to move beyond basic data visualization and make data-driven decisions that can lead to improved performance and achieve better results.

Automation of Repetitive Tasks

Microsoft Copilot dives into the realm of automation, freeing you from repetitive tasks within the Microsoft 365 suite and empowering you to focus on higher-value work. Here's how Copilot streamlines your workflow across various applications:

Effortless Data Manipulation:

- **Excel Automation:** Copilot can automate repetitive tasks in Excel, such as data formatting, cleaning, and transformation. Imagine automatically converting dates to a specific format (like in the picture below), removing duplicates, or extracting critical data points – all at the click of a button or with a defined prompt.

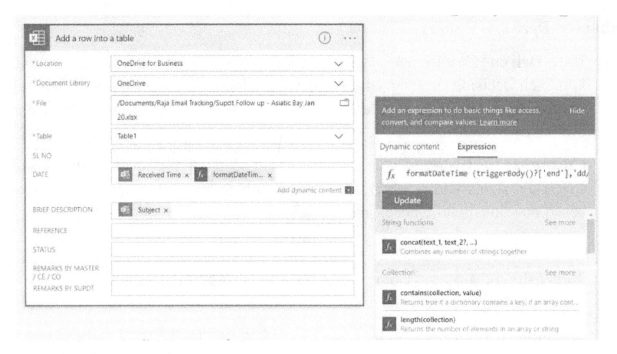

- **Automated Report Generation:** Struggling with generating repetitive reports? Copilot can learn your report structure and automate the process based on your data. This frees you up to focus on data analysis and insights, while Copilot handles the tedious aspects of report creation.

Streamlined Communication and Collaboration:

- **Automating Emails:** Dreading repetitive emails? Craft a template with placeholders, and Copilot can personalize it with specific information for each recipient (like names and deadlines), saving you significant time and effort.

- **Meeting Agendas and Notes:** Generate basic meeting agendas or summarize key takeaways and action items from your meetings automatically with Copilot. This ensures everyone stays on the same page and eliminates the need for manual note-taking.

Enhanced Organization and Productivity:

- **Schedule Management:** Copilot can analyse your workload and suggest ways to optimize your schedule. It might identify opportunities to reschedule meetings or automate tasks, ensuring you have dedicated time for focused work.

- **Customizable Automations:** Copilot allows you to create custom automation rules based on your specific needs. Let's say you frequently attach a standard legal disclaimer to specific types of emails. Copilot can learn this pattern and automate the attachment process, ensuring compliance and saving you time.

Remember:

- Explore the automation functionalities within each Microsoft 365 application to discover the specific tasks Copilot can automate for you.

- Provide clear instructions and examples when setting up custom automations to ensure Copilot executes them according to your requirements.

By leveraging Microsoft Copilot's automation capabilities, you can significantly reduce the time spent on repetitive tasks within the Microsoft 365 environment. This frees up valuable time and mental energy, allowing you to focus on strategic initiatives and drive greater productivity.

Natural Language Processing Capabilities

Microsoft Copilot shines in its ability to understand and process natural language. This empowers you to interact with it using clear and concise instructions, allowing Copilot to assist you in various tasks within the Microsoft 365 ecosystem. Here's how Copilot leverages natural language processing (NLP) to enhance your workflow:

Intuitive Prompt-Based Interaction:

- **Clear Communication:** Forget complex coding or scripting. Interact with Copilot through natural language prompts. Tell Copilot what you want it to do, whether it's summarizing a document, creating a data chart in Excel, or composing an email in a specific tone.

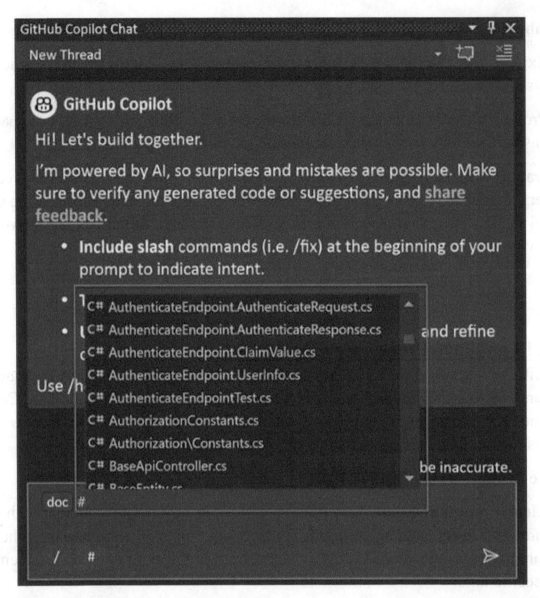

GitHub Copilot Chat

New Thread

GitHub Copilot

Hi! Let's build together.

I'm powered by AI, so surprises and mistakes are possible. Make sure to verify any generated code or suggestions, and share feedback.

- **Include slash** commands (i.e. /fix) at the beginning of your prompt to indicate intent.

C# AuthenticateEndpoint.AuthenticateRequest.cs
C# AuthenticateEndpoint.AuthenticateResponse.cs
C# AuthenticateEndpoint.ClaimValue.cs
C# AuthenticateEndpoint.UserInfo.cs
C# AuthenticateEndpointTest.cs
C# AuthorizationConstants.cs
C# Authorization\Constants.cs
C# BaseApiController.cs

and refine

Use /h

be inaccurate.

doc #

/ #

- **Contextual Understanding:** Copilot goes beyond just understanding individual words. It analyses the context of your prompts and the surrounding information within your Microsoft 365 applications to provide the most relevant and helpful response.

Generating Different Creative Text Formats:

- **Content Creation at Your Fingertips:** Struggling to start a creative writing project? Provide Copilot with a starting sentence or a brief description of your idea, and it can generate different creative text formats, like poems, code, scripts, musical pieces, and more, to spark your inspiration.

- **Tailored Writing Styles:** Need to write in a specific tone or style? Instruct Copilot accordingly, and it will craft content that adheres to your guidelines. This can be particularly helpful for marketing copy, social media posts, or business reports.

Seamless Communication and Translation:

- **Real-time Translation:** Communicate effortlessly with colleagues or clients around the world. Copilot can translate emails, messages, or documents in real-time, ensuring clear and efficient communication across language barriers.

- **Summarizing Key Points:** Copilot can analyse lengthy documents, emails, or meeting transcripts and provide concise summaries of the key points. This saves you time and allows you to quickly grasp the essential information.

Remember:

- The more you interact with Copilot using natural language, the better it understands your preferences and communication style.

- Experiment with different prompts and phrasing to discover the range of functionalities Copilot offers within each Microsoft 365 application.

By leveraging Microsoft Copilot's natural language processing capabilities, you can bridge the gap between human and machine interaction within the Microsoft 365 environment. This allows you to interact with Copilot in a way that feels natural and intuitive, ultimately boosting your productivity and achieving more with less effort.

CHAPTER FOUR
USING TO MICROSOFT COPILOT IN DIFFERENT APPLICATIONS

Microsoft Word

Microsoft Word is where Microsoft Copilot truly shines as your intelligent writing companion. By leveraging natural language processing (NLP), Copilot understands the context of your work and responds to your instructions in plain English. This empowers you to write more efficiently, overcome writer's block, and generate creative text formats, all within the familiar Word interface.

Effortless Writing Assistance:

- **Real-time Suggestions:** As you type, Copilot analyses your sentences and paragraphs, offering suggestions for grammar, style, and phrasing. Imagine you're writing a report and unsure about a specific word choice. Copilot can provide synonyms or suggest alternative phrasings that better convey your intended meaning.

- **Contextual Completions:** Copilot goes beyond basic suggestions. It analyses the surrounding text and provides contextually relevant completions for sentences, paragraphs, or even entire sections. For instance, you might start a sentence with "The meeting addressed the importance of..." Copilot can suggest completions like "customer satisfaction" or "meeting deadlines," depending on the context of your document.

- **Overcoming Writer's Block:** Hitting a wall and struggling to move forward with your writing? Provide Copilot with a starting sentence or topic, and it can generate different creative text formats to jumpstart your ideas. This could be anything from simple outlines or bullet points to full-fledged creative writing prompts in various styles.

Natural Language Interaction:

- **Prompt-Based Content Creation:** Instead of complex menus or buttons, interact with Copilot using natural language prompts. Simply tell Copilot what you want it to do, whether it's "Write a persuasive introduction for this cover letter" or "Summarize the key takeaways of this section." The more you interact with Copilot in this way, the better it tailors its responses to your writing style and preferences.

- **Refine and Adapt:** Copilot's suggestions are a starting point, not the final product. Review them carefully, accept or modify them as needed, and provide feedback through upvotes or downvotes to help Copilot learn and improve its future suggestions for you.

Beyond Text - Research and Information Retrieval:

- **Intelligent Search:** Stuck searching for relevant information within your Word document or across other Microsoft 365 applications? Utilize Copilot's natural language processing to find the information you need quickly and efficiently. Formulate your search query in plain English, and Copilot can search your documents and provide relevant excerpts or data points.

By harnessing the power of Microsoft Copilot within Microsoft Word, you can transform your writing experience. From real-time assistance and overcoming writer's block to leveraging natural language interaction and information retrieval, Copilot empowers you to write with more confidence, efficiency, and creativity.

Microsoft Excel

Microsoft Excel is a powerhouse for data analysis, and Microsoft Copilot takes it a step further. By leveraging Copilot's AI capabilities, you can unlock hidden insights in your spreadsheets, automate repetitive tasks, and generate data visualizations with greater ease. Here's how Copilot elevates your Excel experience:

Unveiling Data Insights:

- **Intelligent Data Analysis:** Copilot analyses your spreadsheet data to identify trends, patterns, and outliers you might not have noticed on your own. It can highlight these insights and suggest relevant charts or graphs to visualize them effectively, transforming raw data into actionable information.

- **Ask and Explore:** Move beyond static data tables. Interact with Copilot using natural language prompts like "Show me the sales trends by region over the past year" or "What factors contribute to the increase in customer churn?" Copilot will analyse your data and generate clear explanations or visualizations based on your questions.

- **Predictive Analytics:** Harness the power of Copilot's AI to forecast future trends. Provide historical data sets, and Copilot can identify patterns and predict future outcomes, empowering you to make data-driven decisions and plan for upcoming scenarios.

Effortless Data Manipulation:

- **Automated Tasks:** Streamline your workflow by automating repetitive tasks in Excel. Copilot can handle data cleaning, formatting, and transformation, freeing you up to focus on more analytical work. Imagine automatically removing duplicates, converting data types, or enriching your data from external sources – all at the click of a button or with a defined prompt.

- **Formula Generation:** Struggling to write complex formulas? Describe what you want to achieve with your data, and Copilot can suggest the appropriate formulas to perform the calculations. This is particularly helpful for beginners or when working with unfamiliar functions.

- **Customizable Automation:** Copilot allows you to create custom automation rules based on your specific needs. For instance, you can set up rules to automatically format specific data sets or generate charts whenever new data is imported.

Enhanced Data Visualization:

- **Intelligent Chart Recommendations:** Not sure which chart type best represents your data? Copilot analyses your data and suggests suitable chart formats, like bar charts for comparisons or line charts for trends. This ensures you choose the most effective way to visually communicate your findings.

- **Interactive Data Exploration:** Go beyond static charts. Leverage Copilot to create interactive dashboards that allow you to drill down into specific data points and explore your data from different perspectives. This fosters deeper data analysis and helps you uncover hidden patterns or relationships within your data sets.

Remember:

- Explore Copilot's functionalities within the Excel ribbon or by using natural language prompts within your spreadsheets.

- The more you utilize Copilot's data analysis and automation features, the better it understands your work style and data patterns, leading to more relevant and personalized suggestions in the future.

By incorporating Microsoft Copilot into your Excel workflow, you can unlock the full potential of your data. From intelligent analysis and automated tasks to enhanced data visualization, Copilot empowers you to gain deeper insights, make data-driven decisions, and ultimately achieve better results.

Microsoft PowerPoint

Microsoft PowerPoint is a cornerstone tool for creating impactful presentations. However, crafting engaging slides and weaving data into a captivating story can be time-consuming. Here's where Microsoft Copilot steps in, becoming your intelligent partner in crafting presentations that resonate with your audience.

Effortless Content Creation:

- **Transform Text into Slides:** Struggling to translate your notes or outlines into compelling slides? Provide Copilot with your existing content, and it can automatically generate draft slides with proper formatting, structure, and bullet points. This saves you time spent manually creating slides and allows you to focus on refining the content.

- **AI-powered Storytelling:** Data is crucial, but presentations are about telling a story. Copilot analyses your content and data sets to identify key themes and suggest a narrative flow for your presentation. This ensures your slides are well-organized, follow a logical progression, and effectively guide your audience through your message.

- **Content Curation and Citation:** Need to incorporate relevant data or visuals into your slides but short on time? Provide Copilot with keywords or topics related to your presentation, and it can search reliable sources and suggest relevant content or royalty-free images to enhance your slides.

Enhanced Visual Appeal:

- **Intelligent Design Suggestions:** Unsure about design choices? Copilot can analyse your content and suggest design elements like layouts, fonts, and colour palettes that complement your message and resonate with your target audience. This ensures your presentation is visually appealing and professional-looking.

- **Data Visualization Made Easy:** Don't just list data points – tell a visual story. Copilot can analyse your data and recommend suitable chart formats or data visualizations to effectively convey your findings. Imagine converting raw data tables into impactful charts or graphs with just a few clicks or a natural language prompt.

- **Automated Slide Transitions:** Ensure a smooth flow between your slides with Copilot's automated transition suggestions. This removes the need to manually configure transitions for each slide, saving you time and creating a more polished presentation experience.

Seamless Collaboration and Delivery:

- **Real-time Collaboration:** Working on a presentation with a team? Copilot can facilitate real-time collaboration within PowerPoint. Team members can add comments, suggestions, or edits directly within the presentation, ensuring everyone stays on the same page and contributes effectively.

- **Speaker Notes Generation:** Struggling to summarize key points for your speaker notes? Copilot can analyse your slides and automatically generate concise speaker notes that highlight the main takeaways of each slide. This allows you to focus on delivering a captivating presentation without relying solely on memorization.

Remember:

- Explore Copilot's functionalities within the PowerPoint ribbon or interact with it through natural language prompts while working on your slides.

- The more you utilize Copilot's content creation and design features, the better it understands your presentation style and preferences, leading to more relevant suggestions and a more streamlined workflow in the future.

By leveraging Microsoft Copilot's capabilities within PowerPoint, you can transform the way you create presentations. From effortless content creation and storytelling to enhanced visuals and seamless collaboration, Copilot empowers you to craft impactful presentations that engage your audience and deliver your message with clarity and impact.

Microsoft Outlook

Microsoft Copilot seamlessly integrates with Microsoft Outlook, your central hub for email communication. Let's explore how Copilot streamlines your workflow and elevates your email interactions:

Effortless Email Creation:

- **Craft Compelling Emails:** Dreading writing lengthy or complex emails? Copilot can assist you in crafting effective emails. Provide a brief description of the email's purpose and recipient, and Copilot can suggest greetings, closings, body paragraphs, or even entire email structures tailored to the specific situation.

- **Real-time Grammar and Style Check:** Similar to Word, Copilot offers real-time suggestions for grammar, style, and phrasing within your emails. This ensures your message is clear, concise, and professional.

- **Overcoming Writer's Block:** Stuck formulating an email and unsure how to proceed? Provide Copilot with a starting sentence or topic, and it can generate different creative text formats to spark your ideas. This could be anything from email outlines to suggested talking points, helping you overcome writer's block and get your message across effectively.

Enhanced Communication and Collaboration:

- **Real-time Translation:** Working with international colleagues or clients? Copilot can translate emails in real-time, fostering seamless communication and collaboration across language barriers. No more waiting for translations or struggling to communicate your message clearly.

- **Meeting Agendas and Follow-ups:** Hectic schedule and struggling to keep track of meeting details? Leverage Copilot to generate basic meeting agendas before your meetings and summarize key takeaways and action items afterward. This ensures everyone stays on the same page and keeps projects moving forward.

Improved Organization and Productivity:

- **Automated Email Drafts:** For repetitive emails with a standard format, create a template with placeholders. Copilot can personalize these templates with specific information for each recipient, saving you significant time and effort.

- **Smart Search Functionality:** Utilize Copilot's natural language processing to search your inbox and files more efficiently. Formulate your search query in plain English, and Copilot can locate relevant emails, attachments, or data points within your Microsoft 365 environment.

Remember:

- Explore Copilot's functionalities within the Outlook interface. Look for icons or buttons that trigger Copilot's assistance, or interact with it through natural language prompts within your email drafts.

- The more you utilize Copilot for email tasks, the better it understands your communication style and preferences, leading to more personalized and relevant suggestions over time.

By incorporating Microsoft Copilot into your Outlook workflow, you can streamline email creation, enhance communication and collaboration, and ultimately save valuable time to focus on more strategic tasks.

CHAPTER FIVE
ADVANCED FUNCTIONALITIES

Customizing Copilot's Suggestions

Microsoft Copilot allows you to customize its suggestions to better fit your needs. Here's how to do it with pictures:

1. Open the Copilot Settings

Click on the three dots (⋯) in the Copilot pane and select "Settings" or press Ctrl+Shift+Alt+S.

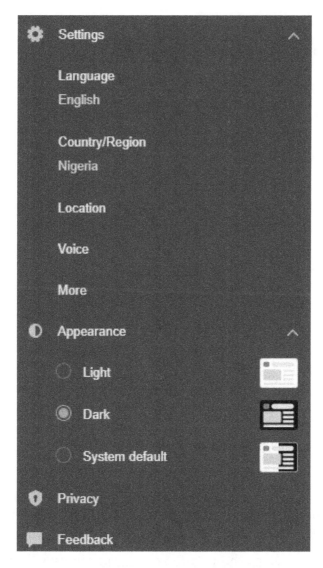

2. Select "Image Settings"

In the settings menu, click on "Image Settings" to access the image customization options.

3. Choose Your Preferred Image Source

Select your preferred image source from the dropdown menu:

- **Microsoft Bing Images**
- **Microsoft Clipart**
- **Your Organization's Image Library** (if available)

4. Set Image Size and Quality

Adjust the image size and quality to your liking:

- **Image Size**: Choose from Small, Medium, Large, or Custom
- **Image Quality**: Select from Low, Medium, High, or Best

5. Customize Image Styles

Choose from various image styles, such as:

- **Photography**
- **Illustrations**
- **Icons**
- **Clipart**

6. Save Your Changes

Click "Save" to apply your custom image settings.

Now, when you use Copilot, it will suggest images based on your preferred settings, making it easier to find the perfect image for your content.

Example:

Suppose you're creating a presentation about wildlife conservation. With Copilot's customized image settings, you can set your preferred image source to "Microsoft Bing Images," select "Photography" as the image style, and choose "Large" image size. Copilot will then suggest high-quality wildlife photos from Bing Images to illustrate your points.

Integrating Third-Party Applications

Microsoft Copilot supports integration with various third-party applications, enhancing its capabilities and streamlining workflows. Here's how to integrate third-party apps with Copilot:

1. Access the Copilot Store

Click on the "Apps" icon in the Copilot pane or press Ctrl+Shift+Alt+A.

2. Browse the Copilot Store

Search for third-party apps in the store, such as:

- **Trello**
- **Asana**
- **Google Drive**
- **Dropbox**

3. Install the App

Click the "Install" button next to the app you want to integrate.

4. Authorize the App

Grant Copilot permission to access the third-party app by following the authorization prompts.

5. Configure the App

Set up the app integration by following the instructions provided by Copilot.

6. Start Using the Integrated App

Once configured, you can access the third-party app directly from Copilot, leveraging its features and functionality within your workflow.

Benefits of Integration:

- **Streamlined workflows**
- **Enhanced productivity**
- **Seamless access to third-party app features**
- **Improved collaboration and organization**

By integrating third-party applications with Microsoft Copilot, you can expand its capabilities, automate tasks, and boost your productivity.

Utilizing Copilot's API for Developers

Microsoft Copilot provides an API for developers to integrate its advanced AI capabilities into their applications, enabling them to build innovative solutions. Here's how to utilize Copilot's API:

1. Register for a Developer Account

Sign up for a Microsoft developer account to access the Copilot API.

2. Obtain an API Key

Generate an API key from the Microsoft Azure portal.

3. Choose the API Endpoint

Select the appropriate API endpoint for your application:

- **Text API**: For text-based applications

- **Speech API**: For speech-based applications

- **Image API**: For image-based applications

4. Use the API

Make API calls to Copilot using your preferred programming language, such as Python, Java, or C#.

5. Integrate Copilot's Capabilities

Leverage Copilot's AI capabilities, including:

- **Language understanding**

- **Text generation**

- **Speech recognition**

- **Image analysis**

Benefits for Developers:

- **Access to advanced AI capabilities**

- **Flexibility to build innovative applications**

- **Streamlined development process**

- **Enhanced user experience**

By utilizing Copilot's API, developers can create powerful applications that harness the potential of AI, driving innovation and growth in various industries.

Example:

A developer builds a chatbot using Copilot's API, enabling users to ask questions and receive accurate answers. The chatbot leverages Copilot's language understanding and text generation capabilities, providing a seamless user experience.

CHAPTER SIX
SECURITY AND PRIVACY CONSIDERATIONS

Data Privacy Policies

Microsoft Copilot adheres to strict data privacy policies, ensuring the secure collection, storage, and use of user data. Here are the key aspects of Copilot's data privacy policies:

1. Data Collection

Copilot collects user data only when necessary for providing services, such as:

- **User authentication**
- **Usage patterns**
- **Error reporting**

2. Data Storage

Collected data is stored securely in Microsoft's servers, adhering to industry standards for data protection.

3. Data Use

User data is used solely for:

- **Improving Copilot's services**
- **Enhancing user experience**
- **Ensuring compliance with legal obligations**

4. Data Protection

Microsoft implements robust security measures to protect user data from:

- **Unauthorized access**
- **Disclosure**
- **Alteration**
- **Deletion**

5. Data Retention

User data is retained only for as long as necessary to provide services or as required by law.

6. User Rights

Users have the right to:

- **Access their data**
- **Rectify inaccurate data**
- **Request data deletion**
- **Object to data processing**

7. Compliance with Regulations

Copilot complies with major data privacy regulations, including:

- **General Data Protection Regulation (GDPR)**
- **California Consumer Privacy Act (CCPA)**
- **Data Protection Act (DPA)**

By adhering to these data privacy policies, Microsoft Copilot ensures the secure and responsible handling of user data, maintaining trust and confidence in its services.

<u>Security Measures and Compliance</u>

Microsoft Copilot prioritizes security and compliance, implementing robust measures to protect user data and ensure adherence to industry standards and regulations. Here are the key security measures and compliance initiatives:

Security Measures:

- **Encryption**: Data is encrypted in transit and at rest using industry-standard protocols.
- **Access Control**: Multi-factor authentication, secure login, and role-based access control ensure only authorized access.
- **Data Centres**: Copilot's data centres are ISO 27001 certified, with 24/7 monitoring and robust physical security.
- **Network Security**: Firewalls, intrusion detection, and prevention systems protect against unauthorized access.

- **Regular Security Updates**: Continuous monitoring and patching ensure the latest security fixes.

Compliance Initiatives:

- **SOC 2**: Copilot meets Service Organization Control (SOC) 2 standards for security, availability, and confidentiality.

- **ISO 27001**: Copilot's information security management system is ISO 27001 certified.

- **GDPR**: Copilot complies with the General Data Protection Regulation (GDPR) for EU user data.

- **HIPAA**: Copilot meets Health Insurance Portability and Accountability Act (HIPAA) standards for healthcare data.

- **CCPA**: Copilot complies with the California Consumer Privacy Act (CCPA) for California user data.

Additional Measures:

- **Regular Security Audits**: Independent third-party audits ensure Copilot's security posture.

- **Incident Response**: Established procedures for responding to security incidents.

- **Employee Training**: Regular security awareness training for employees.

By implementing these security measures and complying with industry regulations, Microsoft Copilot ensures the confidentiality, integrity, and availability of user data.

Managing Permissions and Access

Microsoft Copilot provides robust permission and access management features to ensure that users only have access to the resources and data they need to perform their tasks. Here are the key features:

Permission Levels:

- **Owner**: Full control over resources and data

- **Contributor**: Edit and contribute to resources and data

- **Reader**: Read-only access to resources and data

Access Control:

- **Role-Based Access Control (RBAC)**: Assign roles to users to determine access levels

- **Attribute-Based Access Control (ABAC)**: Grant access based on user attributes and environmental conditions

Resource Permissions:

- **Files and Folders**: Control access to specific files and folders

- **Applications**: Manage access to Copilot applications and features

- **Data**: Regulate access to sensitive data and information

User Management:

- **User Profiles**: Create and manage user profiles with specific permissions and access levels

- **User Groups**: Organize users into groups for easier permission management

- **User Authentication**: Integrate with Azure Active Directory (AAD) or other authentication systems

Permission Inheritance:

- **Inherit permissions from parent resources**

- **Override inherited permissions for specific resources**

By utilizing these permission and access management features, administrators can effectively manage user access and ensure the security and integrity of resources and data within Microsoft Copilot.

CHAPTER SEVEN
TROUBLESHOOTING AND SUPPORT

Common Issues and Solutions

Here are some common issues you might encounter with Microsoft Copilot and solutions to address them:

- **Limited Technical Proficiency:** Users with limited computer literacy might find Copilot's interface or functionalities challenging.

- **Solution:** Microsoft could provide more comprehensive tutorials, in-app guidance, and user-friendly interfaces to enhance accessibility.

- **Subscription Model:** Copilot is currently part of paid Microsoft 365 subscriptions, limiting accessibility for some users.

- **Solution:** Microsoft could explore offering a freemium model with basic Copilot functionalities or integrate Copilot into specific applications for wider adoption.

- **Accuracy of Suggestions:** Copilot suggestions might not always be accurate or aligned with user intent, leading to errors.

- **Solution:** Microsoft can improve Copilot's training data and algorithms to refine suggestion accuracy and allow users to provide feedback for continuous improvement.

- **Overreliance on Copilot:** Overreliance on Copilot for code completion or content generation could hinder creativity or critical thinking skills.

- **Solution:** Users should be encouraged to leverage Copilot as a productivity tool while maintaining a balance with independent problem-solving and creative thinking.

- **Privacy Concerns:** Some users might be apprehensive about an AI assistant accessing their data across Microsoft 365 applications.

- **Solution:** Microsoft can ensure transparency regarding data usage and provide robust privacy controls allowing users to manage their data access preferences. Additionally, clear communication about data anonymization practices can build trust.

- **Bias in Suggestions:** Copilot's suggestions could reflect biases present in its training data, leading to skewed or discriminatory outputs.

- **Solution:** Microsoft can implement bias detection and mitigation techniques during Copilot's training and development. This might involve using diverse datasets and algorithms that identify and minimize potential biases.

- **Security Risks:** Integration of an AI assistant introduces potential security vulnerabilities.

- **Solution:** Microsoft should prioritize robust security measures to protect user data and prevent unauthorized access. Regular security audits and updates are crucial to maintain a secure environment.

- **Ethical Considerations:** The use of AI for content creation raises ethical concerns around plagiarism and originality.

- **Solution:** Microsoft can implement features that promote responsible use of Copilot's content generation capabilities. This could include clear attribution guidelines and encouraging users to use Copilot as a springboard for their own creative work.

- **Limited Customization:** Copilot might not offer enough customization options for users with specific workflows or preferences.

- **Solution:** Microsoft could explore ways for users to personalize Copilot's functionalities to better suit their individual needs and working styles. This might involve allowing users to adjust suggestion settings or prioritize specific types of assistance.

Accessing Support Resources

There are several ways to access support resources for Microsoft Copilot:

- **Microsoft 365 Help Centre:** Search for "Copilot" in the Help Centre for comprehensive articles, tutorials, and FAQs that address frequently encountered issues and basic troubleshooting steps.

- **Microsoft Copilot Lab:** This is a great starting point for exploring Copilot's functionalities and features. The Lab offers helpful articles, training videos, and ready-made prompts to experiment with and get comfortable using Copilot in various scenarios.

- **Microsoft Community Forums:** The Microsoft community forums provide a platform to connect with other Copilot users and Microsoft support personnel.

Search for threads related to your specific issue or ask a new question to get help from the community.

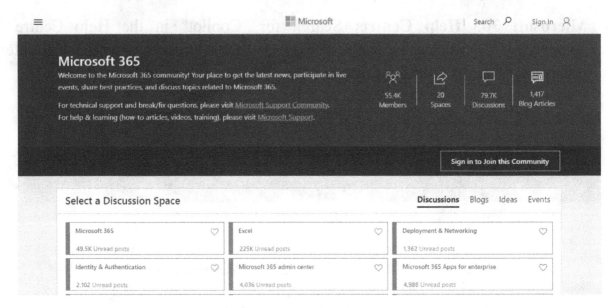

- **Admin Support (for Microsoft Copilot Studio):** If you're an administrator for Microsoft Copilot Studio, you can leverage the Microsoft Power Platform admin centre to request support from Microsoft. This option is suited for technical issues or configuration challenges specific to Copilot Studio.

Remember, the specific support channel you choose might depend on the nature of your query and your administrative role within your organization.

Community and Forums

Here are some community resources where you can connect with other Microsoft Copilot users and get help:

- **Stack Overflow:** Stack Overflow is a popular question-and-answer platform for developers. Search for questions and discussions tagged with 'microsoft-copilot' to find solutions to specific coding problems or general discussions about Copilot's functionalities.

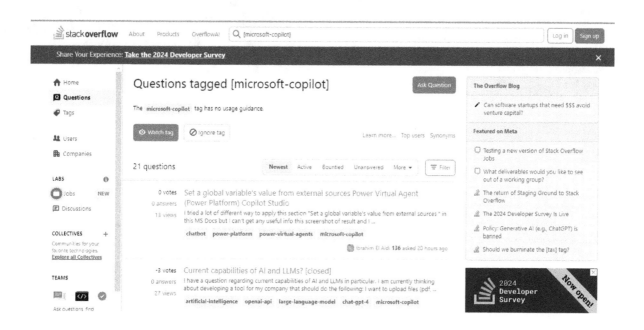

Remember, these are general community forums, so the level of expertise may vary. However, they can be a great way to learn from others and find solutions to common Copilot challenges.

CHAPTER EIGHT
BEST PRACTICES FOR MAXIMIZING PRODUCTIVITY

Tips and Tricks

Microsoft Copilot can be a powerful tool to supercharge your workflow within the Microsoft 365 ecosystem. Here are some tips and tricks to help you get the most out of it:

Sharpen Your Prompting Skills:

- **Think of Copilot as Your Assistant:** Provide clear and concise instructions, just like you would to a colleague. The more context you give, the better Copilot can understand your intent and generate helpful responses.

- **Start with Simple Prompts:** Don't overwhelm Copilot with overly complex requests. Begin with basic prompts and gradually add more details as you refine your desired outcome.

- **Embrace the Power of "Magic Words":** A little politeness goes a long way! Starting prompts with "please" and including "thank you" can encourage positive language patterns and improve Copilot's overall responsiveness over time.

- **Specificity is Key:** The more specific your prompts, the more accurate and relevant Copilot's suggestions will be. For example, instead of saying "Write an email," specify the recipient, purpose, and desired tone.

Fine-tune for Your Workflow:

- **Leverage the Power of Settings:** Explore the Copilot settings to customize its behaviour according to your preferences. You can adjust the tone (formal, informal, etc.), output length, and how strictly it adheres to your company's style guidelines.

- **Become a Prompting Pro:** Practice crafting effective prompts through trial and error. There are various online resources and the Microsoft Copilot Lab that offer prompt examples and guidance for different scenarios.

Unlock Collaboration and Communication Features:

- **Break Down Language Barriers:** Utilize Copilot's translation feature to overcome language barriers in your communication. This can be particularly helpful when working with international teams within Microsoft Teams or Outlook.

- **Summarize Meetings for Action:** Save time after meetings by letting Copilot summarize key takeaways and action items. This ensures everyone is on the same page and facilitates efficient follow-up.

- **Craft Compelling Emails:** Copilot can assist you in drafting emails by suggesting replies, introductions, or even complete email structures.

Remember:

- **Copilot is a Tool, Not a Replacement:** While Copilot offers powerful suggestions, it shouldn't replace your critical thinking and creativity. Use it to enhance your work, not to automate it entirely.

- **Maintain a Critical Eye:** Always review Copilot's suggestions before implementing them. Ensure the code is accurate, the content aligns with your message, and the tone is appropriate.

By following these tips and tricks, you can transform Microsoft Copilot from a helpful assistant into a productivity powerhouse within your Microsoft 365 environment.

Case Studies and Success Stories

While Microsoft Copilot is a relatively new tool, there are emerging examples of its successful application across various industries:

- **Streamlined Sales Operations:** Sales teams at Avanade leverage Copilot within Dynamics 365 to automate tasks like updating contact records and summarizing email threads. This frees up valuable time for them to focus on building relationships and closing deals.

- **Enhanced Financial Services:** Financial institutions like PNB and AmBank utilize Copilot to streamline employee searches and improve the quality of their work. Copilot helps them identify the most qualified candidates and ensures strong communication within their teams.

- **Data-Driven Decision Making:** A manufacturing company used Copilot to analyse data in Excel, uncovering hidden trends in production efficiency. This enabled them to optimize their processes and make data-driven decisions for better resource allocation.

- **Improved Communication and Collaboration:** A global research organization uses Copilot to collaborate on projects across different teams and locations. Copilot facilitates communication by translating languages and summarizing meeting notes, ensuring everyone stays informed and aligned.

Finding More Success Stories:

While there aren't yet centralized repositories specifically for Copilot success stories, you can explore these resources to discover more use cases:

- **Microsoft AI Customer Stories:** This Microsoft webpage showcases customer success stories across various AI products, including some that might involve Copilot within the Microsoft 365 suite.

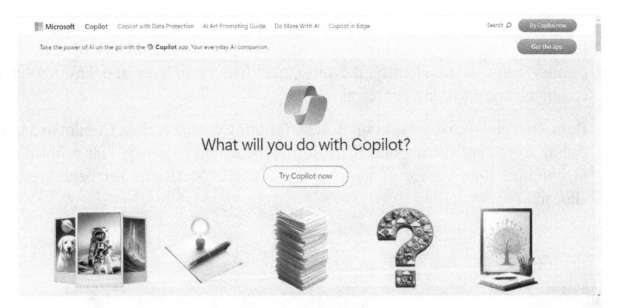

- **Industry Publications and Blogs:** Search for articles or blog posts related to Microsoft Copilot within your specific industry. You might find case studies or testimonials highlighting real-world applications in your field.

- **Social Media Platforms:** Look for relevant discussions or communities focused on Microsoft 365 or productivity tools. Users might share their experiences and success stories with Copilot on platforms like LinkedIn or Twitter.

By exploring these resources, you can gain valuable insights into how different organizations are leveraging Microsoft Copilot to achieve their goals and enhance their workflows.

Continuous Learning and Updates

Microsoft Copilot is designed for continuous learning and improvement, aiming to become a more effective and versatile assistant over time. Here's how Microsoft approaches this:

1. User Feedback and Data:

- **Feedback Mechanisms:** Microsoft integrates various mechanisms within Copilot to collect user feedback. This might involve options to upvote/downvote suggestions, report inaccurate information, or provide written comments on specific outputs.

- **Learning from User Interactions:** Copilot analyses how users interact with its suggestions. This includes observing which suggestions are accepted, rejected, or modified. By understanding user preferences, Copilot can refine its future outputs to better align with user intent.

2. Improved Training Data:

- **Continuously Evolving Data Sets:** Microsoft is likely incorporating new data sources and expanding existing datasets used to train Copilot's underlying AI models. This ensures Copilot stays up-to-date with current trends, language patterns, and technical syntax.

- **Focus on Diversity and Inclusion:** Microsoft strives to include diverse data sources in Copilot's training to mitigate bias and ensure its suggestions are comprehensive and representative.

3. Algorithmic Enhancements:

- **Machine Learning Refinement:** Microsoft researchers are constantly working on improving the machine learning algorithms that power Copilot. This involves optimizing algorithms for better accuracy, reducing errors, and generating more creative and human-like text formats.

- **Focus on Specific Tasks:** Microsoft might develop specialized algorithms for handling particular tasks within Copilot. For example, one algorithm might focus on code completion, while another optimizes content generation for different writing styles.

Overall, Microsoft aims to create a self-learning loop for Copilot. By incorporating user feedback, diverse training data, and ongoing algorithmic advancements, Copilot should progressively enhance its capabilities and deliver a more personalized and efficient user experience.

CHAPTER NINE
FUTURE OF MICROSOFT COPILOT

Upcoming Features and Enhancements

While specific details about future releases might not be publicly available, here's what we can expect based on recent updates and the roadmap for Microsoft 365:

- **Deeper Integration with Microsoft Graph:** Microsoft Graph is a platform that connects data across various Microsoft 365 applications. Look forward to Copilot leveraging Graph more extensively. This could enable functionalities like:

  - **Personalized Prompts:** Copilot might suggest prompts based on your specific work context and data within Microsoft 365 applications.

  - **Targeted Information Retrieval:** You could use Copilot to ask questions and receive information directly from your Microsoft 365 data, using natural language queries.

- **Enhanced Support for Third-Party Applications:** Copilot might expand its reach beyond core Microsoft 365 apps. Imagine using Copilot within project management tools, design software, or other applications you utilize for work.

- **Customizable Copilot Extensions:** Admins might have more control over customizing Copilot's functionalities for their organization. This could involve creating extensions with specific capabilities tailored to their workflows and data sources.

- **Advanced Personalization:** Expect more options to personalize Copilot's behaviour to your preferences. This could include adjusting the writing style, formality level, and technical jargon used in its suggestions.

- **Focus on Accessibility:** Microsoft might prioritize making Copilot more accessible to users with varying technical skill levels. This could involve improved user interfaces, clearer instructions, and comprehensive tutorials.

By implementing these enhancements, Microsoft aims to solidify Copilot's position as a central AI assistant within the Microsoft 365 ecosystem. It will likely become even more adaptable, personalized, and capable of handling complex tasks across different applications.

Roadmap and Vision

While Microsoft doesn't necessarily disclose a public roadmap for specific features, here's what we can glean about Copilot's vision based on existing features, industry trends, and announcements:

Vision: An All-Encompassing AI Assistant for Knowledge Workers

- **Seamless Integration:** Microsoft envisions Copilot seamlessly woven into the fabric of the Microsoft 365 experience. It should work intuitively across all applications, offering context-aware suggestions and automating repetitive tasks.

- **Personalized Workflows:** Copilot will likely become highly customizable, adapting to individual work styles and preferences. Users can personalize everything from writing style to the level of automation desired.

- **Enhanced Collaboration:** Imagine Copilot facilitating smoother collaboration across teams and locations. It could translate languages in real-time, summarize meetings for all participants, and suggest effective communication strategies.

- **AI-Powered Insights:** Copilot might evolve beyond task automation and delve into data analysis. It could uncover hidden trends within your data, suggest data visualizations, and provide insights to help you make informed decisions.

- **Proactive Approach:** An ideal future for Copilot involves anticipating user needs. It could suggest relevant templates, reports, or data visualizations before you even ask, streamlining your workflow further.

Industry Trends and Expected Alignments

- **Focus on Explainable AI:** As AI transparency becomes increasingly important, Microsoft might prioritize making Copilot's decision-making processes more transparent. This would allow users to understand the rationale behind its suggestions and build trust in its capabilities.

- **Integration with Advanced AI Models:** Expect Copilot to leverage advancements in natural language processing (NLP) and large language models (LLMs) to become even more adept at understanding complex instructions and generating human-quality text formats.

- **Ethical Considerations:** Microsoft will likely address ethical concerns surrounding AI-generated content. This could involve measures to prevent plagiarism, ensure factual accuracy, and mitigate bias in Copilot's suggestions.

Overall, Microsoft's vision for Copilot paints a picture of a powerful and versatile AI assistant that empowers knowledge workers to achieve more within the Microsoft 365 ecosystem. By continuously learning, adapting, and integrating cutting-edge AI models, Copilot has the potential to revolutionize the way we work.

Industry Impact and Trends

Microsoft Copilot's impact on the industry is still unfolding, but here's a glimpse into how it might influence trends in AI-powered productivity tools:

- **Rise of Contextual AI Assistants:** Copilot's success could pave the way for a new generation of AI assistants that are deeply integrated within specific software ecosystems. These assistants would understand the context of your work and offer relevant suggestions within that environment.

- **Focus on User-Centric Design:** As AI tools become more prevalent, user-centric design will be paramount. Microsoft's emphasis on user feedback and customization for Copilot highlights this trend. Future AI assistants will likely prioritize a user-friendly experience and offer high levels of personalization.

- **Democratization of AI for Knowledge Workers:** Copilot's potential to automate tasks and generate content could make AI capabilities more accessible to a broader range of knowledge workers. This could empower individuals who might not have extensive coding experience to leverage AI for improved efficiency.

- **Evolving Role of Human Expertise:** AI tools like Copilot won't replace human expertise entirely. Instead, they might shift the focus towards higher-level thinking and strategic tasks. Humans will need to develop skills in areas like critical analysis, creative problem-solving, and ethical considerations to work effectively alongside AI assistants.

- **Importance of Ethical Frameworks:** The rise of AI-powered content generation raises ethical concerns about plagiarism and potential biases. The success of Copilot, and similar tools, will likely depend on Microsoft's commitment to developing and implementing robust ethical frameworks to ensure responsible use of AI technology.

Additionally, Copilot's influence might extend beyond its core functionalities:

- **Impact on Traditional Software Development:** Copilot's code completion features could influence traditional software development approaches. Programmers might rely more heavily on AI suggestions, potentially leading to faster development cycles and reduced error rates.

- **Evolving Education Landscape:** The rise of AI assistants like Copilot could necessitate changes in how we approach education and workforce training. Educational institutions might need to place a greater emphasis on critical thinking and creative problem-solving skills to complement the evolving role of AI in the workplace.

Overall, Microsoft Copilot represents a significant step towards integrating AI into everyday workflows. While its full impact is yet to be seen, it has the potential to reshape how we interact with technology and redefine the way knowledge workers approach their tasks.

CHAPTER TEN
APPENDICES

Glossary of Terms

Here's a glossary of terms you might have encountered throughout our discussion on Microsoft Copilot:

- **AI (Artificial Intelligence):** A branch of computer science concerned with creating intelligent machines capable of mimicking human cognitive functions.

- **API (Application Programming Interface):** A set of protocols and tools that allow applications to communicate with each other.

- **Data Analysis:** The process of examining, interpreting, and visualizing data to extract meaningful insights.

- **Freemium Model:** A business model where a basic version of a product or service is offered for free, with premium features available for a subscription fee.

- **Large Language Model (LLM):** A type of AI model trained on massive amounts of text data to generate human-quality text, translate languages, write different kinds of creative content, and answer your questions in an informative way.

- **Machine Learning:** A type of AI that allows computers to learn from data without explicit programming.

- **Natural Language Processing (NLP):** A subfield of AI concerned with the interaction between computers and human language.

- **Subscription Model:** A method of providing access to a service or product on a recurring payment basis.

- **Workflow:** A series of tasks completed in a specific order to achieve a goal.

- **Bias:** In AI, bias refers to a prejudice reflected in the outputs of an algorithm, often stemming from the data used to train it. It's crucial to mitigate bias in Copilot to ensure fair and representative suggestions.

- **Code Completion:** A feature in Copilot that suggests lines of code or entire code structures as you type. This can accelerate development and reduce errors.

- **Content Generation:** Copilot can generate different creative text formats like emails, letters, scripts, or marketing copy based on your instructions.

- **In-App Functionality:** This refers to Copilot's direct integration within specific Microsoft 365 applications, providing suggestions and functionalities tailored to that program.

- **Machine Learning Algorithms:** Complex mathematical models that underpin Copilot's capabilities. These algorithms are trained on vast data sets to learn patterns and make intelligent suggestions.

- **Natural Language Queries:** Using natural human language to ask questions or provide instructions to Copilot, instead of relying on complex code or commands.

- **Personalization:** The ability to customize Copilot's behaviour to your preferences. This might involve adjusting the writing style, formality level, or technical jargon used in its suggestions.

- **Privacy Concerns:** The use of an AI assistant like Copilot raises concerns about data privacy. Understanding how Copilot handles your data and ensuring robust security measures are in place is crucial.

- **Prompt:** An instruction or question you provide to Copilot to guide it in generating content or completing tasks. The quality and effectiveness of Copilot's outputs depend heavily on how you craft your prompts.

- **Security Risks:** Integrating AI assistants introduces potential security vulnerabilities. It's essential for Microsoft to prioritize robust security measures to protect user data from unauthorized access.

- **Task Automation:** Copilot can automate repetitive tasks within Microsoft 365 applications, freeing up your time to focus on more complex and strategic work.

- **Training Data:** The massive amount of data used to train Copilot's AI models. The quality and diversity of this data significantly influence Copilot's capabilities and potential biases.

Frequently Asked Questions (FAQs)

General Questions

1. What is the purpose of this document?

This document provides answers to frequently asked questions to help users understand and navigate the system, process, or product more effectively.

2. How can I contact customer support?

You can contact customer support by emailing support@example.com or calling our hotline at (123) 456-7890.

Account Management

3. How do I create an account?

To create an account, click on the "Sign Up" button on the homepage, fill in the required details, and follow the instructions to verify your email address.

4. I forgot my password. How can I reset it?

Click on the "Forgot Password" link on the login page, enter your email address, and follow the instructions sent to your email to reset your password.

5. How can I update my account information?

Log in to your account, go to the "Account Settings" section, and update the necessary information. Make sure to save the changes.

Billing and Payments

6. What payment methods are accepted?

We accept credit/debit cards, PayPal, and bank transfers.

7. How can I view my billing history?

Log in to your account, navigate to the "Billing" section, and you will find your billing history along with detailed invoices.

8. What should I do if my payment is declined?

First, check your payment details for any errors. If everything is correct and the payment is still declined, contact your bank or our customer support for further assistance.

Technical Support

9. How do I report a technical issue?

You can report a technical issue by submitting a support ticket through the "Help Centre" on our website or by emailing support@example.com with a detailed description of the problem.

10. Is there a user manual or guide available?

Yes, a comprehensive user manual is available in the "Help Centre" section of our website. You can also download it in PDF format.

Product Features

11. What are the key features of the product?

Our product offers a range of features including, but not limited to, real-time data analytics, customizable dashboards, and seamless integration with third-party applications.

12. How do I integrate the product with third-party applications?

Refer to the integration guide available in the "Help Centre" for step-by-step instructions on integrating with third-party applications.

Privacy and Security

13. How is my data protected?

We implement advanced encryption protocols and adhere to industry-standard security practices to ensure your data is protected.

14. What is your privacy policy?

Our privacy policy can be found on our website under the "Privacy Policy" section. It details how we collect, use, and protect your personal information.

Miscellaneous

15. Can I provide feedback or suggestions?

Yes, we welcome feedback and suggestions. You can submit them through the "Feedback" section on our website or by emailing feedback@example.com.

16. Where can I find the latest updates and news?

The latest updates and news are posted on our blog and social media channels. You can also subscribe to our newsletter for regular updates.

Additional Resources and Reading Material

To further enhance your understanding and knowledge, we have compiled a list of additional resources and reading materials. These resources cover various topics related to our system, process, or product, and provide in-depth insights and guidance.

General Resources

1. User Manual

A comprehensive user manual is available for download in PDF format. This manual covers all aspects of using our system and provides step-by-step instructions for various functions.

2. Help Centre

Our Help Centre includes articles, FAQs, and tutorials to assist you in resolving common issues and learning more about our product.

Technical Documentation

3. API Documentation

For developers integrating our product with third-party applications, our API documentation provides detailed information on available endpoints, authentication, and usage examples.

4. Integration Guides

Step-by-step guides to help you integrate our product with popular third-party applications and services.

Training and Tutorials

5. Video Tutorials

A series of video tutorials that walk you through the basics and advanced features of our product. These are especially helpful for visual learners.

6. Webinars

Join our live and recorded webinars to get insights from our experts, learn about new features, and participate in Q&A sessions.

Research and Articles

7. White Papers

In-depth white papers authored by our experts, covering various topics related to our industry, technology trends, and best practices.

8. Case Studies

Real-world case studies showcasing how our product has helped clients achieve their goals and solve complex problems.

9. Industry Reports

Access industry reports that provide valuable insights and data on market trends, consumer behaviour, and technological advancements.

Community and Support

10. Community Forums

Join our community forums to connect with other users, share experiences, ask questions, and get support from peers and our team.

11. Customer Support

Our customer support team is always ready to assist you. Visit our support page to find contact information, submit a support ticket, or start a live chat.

External Resources

12. Books and eBooks

A curated list of books and eBooks relevant to our field, including recommended readings for further learning.

13. Online Courses

Enrol in online courses offered by reputable platforms to deepen your understanding and skills.

14. Blogs and Newsletters

Follow industry blogs and subscribe to newsletters to stay updated with the latest trends, news, and insights.

THANK YOU
FOR READING